BURNING THE FURNITURE

ESSENTIAL POETS SERIES 219

BURNING
THE
FURNITURE

paul nelson

GUERNICA
TORONTO – BUFFALO – LANCASTER (U.K.)
2014

Michael Mirolla, editor
Guernica Editions Inc.
P.O. Box 76080, Abbey Market, Oakville, (ON), Canada L6M 3H5
2250 Military Road, Tonawanda, N.Y. 14150-6000 U.S.A.

Distributors:
University of Toronto Press Distribution,
5201 Dufferin Street, Toronto (ON), Canada M3H 5T8
Gazelle Book Services, White Cross Mills, High
Town, Lancaster LA1 4XS U.K.

Book design by Jamie Kerry of Belle Étoile Studios
www.belleetoilestudios.com

First edition.
Printed in Canada.

Legal Deposit – Third Quarter

Library of Congress Catalog Card Number: 2013948331

Library and Archives Canada Cataloguing in Publication
Nelson, Paul, 1934-, author
Burning the furniture / Paul Nelson.

(Essential poets series ; 219)
Poems.
Issued in print and electronic formats.

ISBN 978-1-55071-903-1 (pbk.).--ISBN 978-1-55071-904-8 (epub).--
ISBN 978-1-55071-905-5 (mobi)
I. Title. II. Series: Essential poets series ; 219

PS3564.E483B87 2014   811'.54   C2013-905917-2   C2013-905918-0

CONTENTS

I

II

III

Dedicated with love to my best pals and critics
Jack and Marge Pulaski
Barry and Lorrie Goldensohn

I

Still

as a pickerel in the lilies,
a rainbow finning by a log,
a bass on mud by a green-haired rock,

still as a perched kingfisher in blue
study of what's beneath the surface,
a mink in brown remove, slinking

to curves of littoral, and still
as the overhang of trees,
dripping … or morning moon

waning on the face of a slate pond,
on the face of a boy, having seen these things,
easing shut the screen door,

sure to say nothing,
still as a hatch of mayflies,
dun and sulfur … myriads rising,

drying, flying off, dust
into the shear of swallows
and innocent sun.

Making Me Look

Under spruce and fir, a stream of chartreuse moss,
dented by deer, pawed by bucks in rut, the plot where
twenty years ago I planted two fine dogs.

I haven't been back since, but keep my ears open,
know that glade hasn't been bulldozed or fenced for cattle,
that Olsen's grandson shot his first buck, a ten pointer

within yards of the dogs' remains, as it should be,
magic still wafting like Celtic mist in trees,
the sound of quiet itself, stirring the mind's keep

like a gunshot... dogs barking while I try again
to cherish shadow and fog, seeing them leap fallen logs,
then stand dark against dark, making me look hard.

Snake

Arm deep on gravel in the spiculed spring,
up the still brown slope from the wan farmhouse,
my narrow pal is rapt, garter around a brick,
eyes glassed over,

what I want to do in April, but stride, hot coffee
into the grotto barn to start my gelid engine,
dogs tagging along, coursing ellipses for prey
behind my orange Kubota, diesel

clacking, bushhog whirring, flushing voles, mice
from under clumps of icy hay, scattering
stiff manure, chopping last year's stalks
on swells and flats, a mulch for greening

threat of Spring so fierce that I fear rest,
fear faith as sloughed dusk does me in.
The venerable snake, like this icy circlet,
this galaxy that sunlight "disappears,"

does not believe in me
any more than I do gods
believe me. Even mind me
as I sink in sleep.
My eyes closed rove like dogs.

Just Over There

In shadow waning into mossy dusk
that stump beneath a spruce
could be my mother, or just
a doe rising primly
printing leaves as she steps away
through shreds of light
surprised from her bed by my sweat,
my breath, her ears turned my way

as if she knew me well
mistaking me for friend
the son she always wanted
out of her body, out of her woods

her boy with rifle and knife
come to take flesh from gloom.

She rises vesper hours to clear the fence,
get out of the Old Country,
memories of shelling, soldiers, the fierce
stifling thick of it in a vermin day
into the wide pasture
wide to sharpened stars,
the fresh dark.

She hungers for what's left
of Spring's trace, green, thin blades,
as I get up from the boney ground,
defrocked, disarmed,
passing her in fading haze.

Solace

A long hike pulls me through spruce and birch and time
by a limestone anticline cliffed where the logging road still ends,
leaves another mile of forest to the shore of a shady tarn
set like a black mortar in the inevitable syncline, too cold
to swim in summer, sunlight too small a brass pestle.

Very few have fished there. A mystery how brook trout
got there to thrive on the spring and ice fed oxygen they need
being salmonids, or how I got there once and forever to breathe in
the death-cold solace of obsidian water

a gelid fog in my lungs on hot streets and lots, a tarn
resting in my chest, calm and thoughtless, imagining nothing.

I can do that anytime, sense no magic, or beauty, or peace,
danger or anything else but bottomless self, no place to die
or live but leave alone,

fish just once in a lifetime, releasing the heart's raft, the black
brookies with the bright red spots and orange fins, watching them
slither down beyond sight without gratitude or remembering
a grave presence of mind.

Always After Fire

there's nothing left to take
warped pots limp blades without handles
decent books no photographs
worth taking

We cannot tell the children
We cannot tell them anything
Must not split them into kindling
armloads stacked at the ready
Make them wait like trimmed wicks

when they resort to shadow anyway
play with matches
sensing how parents and tender
adults would burn down the world
to get to the next one
where there's even a circle for suicides
around a smoldering cellar hole
singing "Do not lead me into the valley"

they were sure the children just came from
the muggy punitive womb
And so children want most to be
out nights scuffing in ashes

Casting At Dawn

for my brother, Dave

Back, then forward, pensive arcs
repeated by wrist, his arm
vestigial, line slicing mist,
deliberate, finally released…
… an older guy
at one end of things,

at one with a limber rod,
line shooting the guides,
rolling out like a fleet whip,
the slight leader, faint tippet
lazing, delicately presenting
a dry fly, hackle poised on glassine
that also holds the morning moon,
his tiny sign
set on its fading face.

He knows full well
it is too early, air too damp,
that the sun will come,
stiffen diaphanous wings
by the millions, the lethal world
hatched, a rapture by nine,
clouds of souls flittering up.

He understands that whatever
for the moment lies, finning in gloom
among the rocks on gravel, that
whatever sidles a tumored log,

will also wait for exacting
fate, won't rise now, or leap
for the hell of it, not even
when he begins the retrieve,
foot by foot, the double tapered 4
dividing the pool without a vee.

He wrists the rod tip, tic,
to make the Blue Dun twitch,
rehearsing for the heavy
writhing in his net…

… how else wrest himself
clear of catching something… free
to see his small, hand-tied thing
come back, fret the surface,
safe and exquisite?

Dancing On The Concrete

One stride, another, into the countryside,
street lights arriving like migrants
who knew something, strung out, incandescent
and charged by a glacial god
dammed for decades somewhere
up in the White Mountains.

The poles rose in exclamation,
stretched the new faith past roadside sheds,
past stubble fields to the next township,
by a water-tower below which
homeless cozy by tiny fires.
Farmhouses, miles apart,
shrink from this alien dawn
suffusing the front yards.

Some folk move still further into woods
to live with night again, their faces opalesced
by moonlight, lilac as cadavers, eyes
pixilated in wolfish, wary ways, reflecting
the "Square of Pegasus," the Pleiades,
Ursa Major … frames one might leap through
into everywhere.

Said to be "well armed,"
shape-shifting in and out of light,
edgy as feral dogs, they charmed us kids

who played basketball beneath a light pole
where our fathers had hung a board, hoop and net
lit by one glass bulb, its shade's white underside
battered by ecstatic moths.

We danced on the concrete like chalked aborigines
tossing a pink skull, our shadows
scraps, caressing, fouling each other.

At Dusk

The eastern corner of the field
tans now where I left it, where the sun,
drowning in spruce, at the opposite
end of the universe, leaves last,

where deer leap the wire from sleep,
out of the woods, to browse the sparse green
and be distant, get the most from night.

Is that not what to wish for,
after so many days under sun,
tired, sleepless and ungrateful,
our skins thinning?

Their orange hides wane to somber
like cedar bark, like shadows
where winter's shoulders heave all year.

This is where dogs and the horse
are buried, where I can go myself
when it is time to be cold.

II

String Theory

You see again how far away
Each thing is from every other thing.

— Louise Gluck, "Telescope"

Distance as distances. That is,
until a bit of matter falls from harness
lashing the night sky, and you
move without thought
to pick her up, one strand twining another

such speed and care that lifetimes,
leagues, inches, a hair's breadth
and anything else between
fails to exist and so
the suspicious star in the x-ray,
the black field you walk toward,
ancient mouth in rictus,
dissolves, whole again.

Airivata

De-bungee the blue tarp and let billow
in a flush wish of April wind
this scarf of adolescent sky tossing
last spectral bits of ice

Bundle it sloughed in the lee of trees
leaving the new born hull
glowing on the littoral
afloat on its corroded trailer
half buried in gravel

calling me to mount
peer over into the next world
see my own soul leave my body be
on the crest of the woman who wants me
to fall and rise
launched on the swell of Fundy tide

to take heart in the hardened sail
rigid keel slicing aside
the gray sweater of crocheted weed
rotting ice cakes down from broken lakes

my body reined and naked
chilled under the sailing sun
jib and main
bellowing sheets of music

Ripping The Traps

Back in the house, my woman
gessoes with a broad brush, lightly over,
by my own lights, a flashy herring run,
or sandpipers flaring, collectively,
without grief.

I said she is making fog.
She shook her head,
said her subject is paint.

Across my mowed, soaked field, overnight,
spiders have raised and strung
hundreds of lavender traps on the stubble.
Shuffling dew, I make a black trail
just inside the barbed wire.

Something I missed with the blades
catches my eye, a foot high, stray
balsam, poking above the swathes
without self.
I want to leave it alone,

but if love is waste,
a sachet for sheets in a drawer
to be drawn up over my dead nose,
damn the folded linen! The muslin gouache.
I want the sun's incisive fire to burn the haze.

It's just too early. Too steamed
to see straight. (I wear them for reading.)
I stride toward the house,

obliquely, right through the field,
ripping the snares.
We have to talk.

For Now

The shed high boulder rests
blessed by left-over moon
white in western dawn
as the dirty glacier scouring north
that left this pocket drumlin
magic egg of pale granite
where a woman strips to sun
adorns an Aztec altar
where children pose akimbo
then jump as if drugged into air
down into packets of hay
ringed by sheep that trail shade
like night all day

In Passing

> *I never made the mistake of thinking that I*
> *owned my own strength, that was my secret.*
> *And so I was never alone in my failures.*
>
> — Louise Erdrich, "Nanapush"

I twist my neck in passing
an emerald field lying out
beyond a narrow, tannic, probably toxic river.
It's been a long day; my eyes ache
for the softness, the dusk of it.
Figures in motion there, but I U-turn anyway,
what I do lately,
across a concrete bridge and rumble strip
into the park.

Pewter dusk welds the chain link fence, man high,
beyond which, on the turf, children
commit every sin known to man: side-swiping,
baiting, poaching, fouling, coveting,
spitting and tearing at each other's clothes … above all,
the insanity of laughter.

Simple things, lately, simply transmogrify,
as if all it takes is a ball, any cool spring evening
and a strong fence to invent a game,
any game, The Game, to inspire a local crowd,
the rictus of which still drives me
restless into solitude.

One of the boys looks something like me at that age,
so much so he stalls my sidelong
yearning for his mother
sipping a beer in the splintery stands,
laughing, yelling at the boy to haul up his pants
that keep falling over his half-back hips.
And the wild girl with the mis-matched socks,

snaggle-tooth grin and incendiary hair
who must also be hers, though Mom's
tinted to the dark side now.
I think to say something.
But it is so dangerous today
to speak to children.
Or women.
See, I had an original thought,
once, that things were imperfect. That notion
keeps rolling through the world like a ball
that hits the wire, springs back, always in play,
just beyond my feet … the half-back slicing by, kicking it
without a glance my way. She wouldn't
teach him otherwise. But he will wander.

I don't know if I've truly loved; she
was the only one, four million years
before troubadours, when we left our footprints
in the clay.

O, I bumbled, rambled for eons, intuitions
snarled as caducei, hearing rumors.
She hadn't burned in Carthage; I merely
smelt smoke, astern. She lived among women
on Ithaca. She consorted with Cain.
Washed feet with her hair. Chewed her

fingernails in a convent. Married a local.
Her little boy dodges by, yells "Freak Head" and
runs beneath her, under the stands,
kicking trash.

But, it's a nice evening; I merely need
to stay calm, all of them safe as they can be,
on the soft ground, the chilly grass,
the kids slipping, sliding into it, hilarious.
She stretches, yawns, just beautiful,
teeters for an instant on the bleachers,
the grass blackening, and because I am a stranger,

one of those dreamers in her narrowing,
harrowing eyes, an aspect of dusk
perhaps she remembers like small light
deserting the field, I sidle to my Outback
before my fingers, hooked in the wire,
do the helix thing, turn to ivy.

I Brought Her Thin-Skinned Juicy Lemons

remembering Ken Wlaschin

tumid with recent rains
she will take lemon curd to market
with her pure *lehua* honey

my visit barely citric or syrup
Sister wishes me to pray

the Pacific stretching away
vast blue inkling
below the monastery

She wants to carry my soul like a fragrance
present it to her blue translucent Virgin
floating in glass

this *u'i* Hawaiian whose nostrils flare
at the mustard of my nerves
whose flesh does not belong in words
but Gauguin's sand and red-earth oils
eggplant tint in silk skin
even in overalls

standing under liana vines
that lace the yard's banyan roots
those organ pipes
edging rainforest on Mt. Ka'ala
the vines a screen for what discretion

Elephant leaves listen everywhere
to wind and rain and anybody's prayer
Abbot working budget and sin
twisting in his koa chair by the window

Uphill the simple man-high
bright white cross

my head clearing as breathing eases
the long climb to their sanctuary
Sister offering retreat
in scented ether
a few dollars a day
a strict bed
amber oil lamp
and the warm view toward the invisible
gelid Aleutians

She knows I fear
what I must not fear
what no animal fears

At night so many little windows
Pleiades Orion's Trapezium
the Square of Pegasus
Ursas to leap through

because my traffic's with the living
how Sister can thrive in that body

She has her cell she says and laughs
that I am free to free anyone
with observation of the Galapagos
but cannot free my friend who died last night

Sister wouldn't
married to essence of *lehua*
infusing her will
her innocence
though some say she's been in prison

She'd free him by magic
and sings so

the perched monastery
reeking of flowers
honey sweat horses pigs and hope
chickens running with their chicks
goats nosing my palm
peacocks fanning ridiculous
stained glass tails
Much to fear here
the business of sweetness
that crystallizes with time
like time
that must be heated by Hell
thin to clear belief

Ah Sister what happens when meditation
melts the lead of consolation
and whose life's ever whole consoled

and are they really listening
these huge glistening leaves
those wandering constellations
these hung roots fingering earth
that goat those bees

Ah, your miraculous honey
the infinite black calm in your eyes

I look away
down to riffs of choral surf
scarfing the littoral
the flood-plain town of Waialua
where harried, calm, ordinary lives
and one man's quiet spent
with fine jazz and love's opera
took as long as it takes

Engraved

Air bleak as slate
stiffened her face.
A name there ached.

Some normal economy
of chisel and civil spirit
stored her side by side in stone
with their Colonial boy
locking her in his bed:

Carrie b. 1763 –

No marriage spasmed in the hole
for her, the living dead,
whose people all must know
where each other's bones and souls
lie forever.

Same for this one over here
across the hilled moss
and low-bush cranberry

standing quietly,
straight in a simple shift
print a lily fest,
bluets in the darkening grass
pressed by her sandaled feet
her face flared by sunset
watching her name
to see if it moves
like her shadow.

_____ b. 1963 –

I know this woman's name.
Loved ones want her here,
their small-town plight, the son's

disease more than they can bear
or tricky heat it takes
her to love again
decently some others' boy,

her name engraved,
(no need go close to read it)
let me tell you aches like sleet,
incised where she
breathes at graveside,
jangles car keys, fondles
her mobile phone.

Spring Fault

The wider, gravid river
after tons of upstream rain
writhes this morning like a young body
shedding winter clothes, layers of peat,
branches, trunks spiraling in eddies.
And the wind won't let her think…

… the last virgin
in the big family up the road
watching white caps on the cocoa,
willing to get it over with
under a riven sky where ravens and gulls
wing it like hot uncles
baffled by childish gusts.

She sees the sheep on their knees
have crawled under the shed,
and brand new grass, blown flat,
has stopped whispering.

Bent elders in the neighborhood,
still battened in quilted coats,
take everything as a sign,
rattle their family bones,
poke at the soil, open now, finally,
to burial, their winter losses
stuck to their tongues like wafers

while boys go out without hats
just to hear their brains tear,
zippers, blue nylon jackets
rip from their red flesh.

It's wind, some say; others the river,
or turbid upbringing, too much distraction
and a blistered corpse does float to sea
its eyes open as tokens, a bloated seal, skull

smiling whitely, chopped by a prop
and wallowing along, a beat up
naugahyde cushion, dumb to phenomenal roil…

… a rubber boot, tied off, stuffed with kittens
heaved from the bridge, a rip-tide beginning to sway
beyond the root-beer suds on the marsh,
spring not thinking yet to luff into summer

while Lilith climbs out on the roof
from her bedroom dormer as if
hauling herself on a bed of slippery kelp
to bask in some consuming emotion,
to hunch by frantic surf and air,
thinking about jumping out of her body
into the sea of brand new pungent lilacs
reefed below the eave
where she will never be found.

Adam In March

Bland as Abel with no more story
soul or Saul
I might have lived with animals
giving names to none
or is this maudlin

It's no one's fault that we were young
lovely and easy with our appetites
oblivious to the boom and hiss of noumena
we just couldn't believe
not like lightning or flash floods
so out came the boys
from her muscular womb

I have not known such ecstasy
haven't much character
compared to Jesus
beside himself and deliberate as Cain

Over my eons I've grown vague as faith
living simply in the neighborhood
not far from the ball park
liquor store and post office
fire station and hospital
just a little aside on a dead-end gravel road
like good wine or poetry
by apparent hue and cast
abjure dominion

At night in the woodshed door
talking to galaxies that egos say
strive with the dark

I stand like a cormorant on a rock above tide
wings wide drying and fanning
an old stone gargoyle
pitted by wind rain and reason

I hold up my goblet
swirl then sniff the plum and cassis
the lingering raspberry
sense the tannin the mineral
the bouquet of her child-finished body
a decanter reminding me that I
wasn't born of woman
as Jesus not of man
Popes say

that that is the strength of my celibate soul
to wander just beyond the fold
the viney pale and tangle of women and children
to put up with being rendered
by scholars and maenads
faith-jammed butchers and story tellers
into this or that engendering myth
as they try to eclipse the gibbous moon
glowing weakly on my lawn

My bones have grown porous as coral
with the acid bubbling of thought
my liver-blotched skin "elegant"
as she says "as a leopard"
in the zoo
Do you see me lying there in a cage
growling above a haunch
injected with antibodies
to my own affections

I used to get crazy come May
the soil pinguid as Belgian chocolate
softened and stirred by her
bending in the garden
as if she were global warming

Now March is cruel with quickening
By April there is real heat in the greenhouse
where I strip to sit on a hot wooden chair
brow dripping into a fat novel

There I am one eye out
for isles sirens squalls and tridents
sails albatross or spouts
the other for romaine
tavera beans basil cubanelle Big Boys
that also love this heat
infused with my own mustard vapors
This is not labor
as she undertook the Word
sweat and bled to bring forth death

Not awed by our own voices either
we had no real choices
She picked Cain the egotist
who did the practical thing
with a stone from our soil
dirty bloody medium
and went exiled to Nod
honing his innocence like a scythe
while dangling from the tree of life

She is still so beautiful
but what to do with me if that matters

now I've staggered in
the goat from the hills
my cough ruffling her sanctum
like a garage door opener

as if I've stopped suffering
coma bred of too much allusion
eons of quest elliptically spent
like a ditzy Ulysses

What can she do
burn my stained books
Bear me over the worn sill to the olive bed
Bury my dog

Chaste Norea was not my child
and Lilith (I barely knew the witch)
could not bear children
The Glossary of Terms for Discussion runs
Inspiration Interpretation Intercession
Intercourse with Neighbors
Integrity and Instinct (Jude:19 *who follow mere natural*)
Insight Inherit Increase
but nothing of Incest

Was I not my daughter's first
who has a lump in her cheek this morning
a wad of cotton packing the vacancy
where molar #31 came into the fresh world
and her vision may not get a driver's license
It doesn't look so good now
the garden lined out with string and nothing up
but overnight spicules of heaved frost
waiting out the cold Ides
veiled by winter's scattered wood ash

the old old solo plot
much given to tautology
revision and weeding

I'm a bit like Father now
alone too much and feckless
about the blooming cults

But everything dares grow anyway
in the light of her withering energy
bright as ocular migraine
clots or roses in the bowl
Cain plows it hacks it burns it sacks it
trucks it paves it sells it and Yea
Arugula!
Peas!
Radicchio!
Grapes!

in a gravid murderous world
wrinkled figures on the ground
raisins and sheep shit figs and prunes
crones of Crete who every year
on his birthday haul their black shrouds
to squat and piss on Kazantzakis' grave
dug outside the church yard
for saying He was only human
that he was a Communist
as I eat less exercise and drink the carnal
anti-oxidants of Bordeaux and Argentina
Australia, Chile and South Africa
while watching her ass
and checking my pulse
humming *Hey Jude* or *La Paloma*
worrying stroke awe and enigma

but bright-eyed and wary as a snake
cruising the bog and caught
staring at a toxically gorgeous
golden dart frog

Scythe

I stood my three foot scythe blade
on the haft end
stropping with a gritty stone.
Its edge smiled, the burr
folding over to be swiped again
from the underside, a near
mute shriek of pleasure.

She came to the barn door,
looked on, knew I would make
a carpet around the asparagus bed,
that I loved clearings,
areas trimmed to neat
presences of mind.

Backward, then forward swing,
the heel end of the blade
slightly tipped back, the edge
shearing the low, pale stems
still damp with night, a true
discipline, a meditative act,
no past, no future.

I adore such bullshit.
She knows that, but
when she was alone in the barn
later that morning,
pulling her rake from the corner
she did not see the scythe
quiver on its peg and begin to slide
as if it were not done working.

So quick the way her wrist
turned by instinct down,
nothing in her past to guide her,
no prediction, the blade bouncing
twice on the bone,
making two divots.

I see those scars
gold coins
above the blue veins.

Blood soaked the plank floor.
Flies arrived like neighbors.
Her wrist, gauzed tight and taped,
she sat on a sawhorse, still pale,
shaken but joking, her blood
held again by her body.

Still queasy, I climbed to the loft,
placed the sweet, medieval steel
on three pegs to rust, hang there,
an outworn religion.

The asparagus, like lovers and fools in Spring,
rise green, hearty and nevertheless
through weeds and grass.

Andre The Giant

His work was easy: not to be moved,
to exhaust men against his sides like miners.
Then dine, as he preferred, in his room,
from three carts with three wines.
He would say for grace, C'est mon corps:
C'est mon sang, though his flesh was a legend
he couldn't take and you couldnt leave: "7'4"
580 lbs" printed beneath his barrel face
pasted on how many underpasses,
factories before he came to town?

Kids knew it was an act,
their fathers and mothers and uncles howling,
their spit spraying the ring's apron.
I taped his little finger,
thick as a woman's wrist,
usually sprained on muscled skulls.
He didn't need a last name,
though he passed one on, a daughter ...
... any more than gods.
And he loved his horses.

Floors moved beneath him;
crowds bellowed, parted around him
like bloody water. His routine
was as brief as Saturn's (Goya's),
one head under each arm.
Then he would smile his horse teeth.

Later, he'd duck into a locker room
among the toy bowls

and hunch under the tiny spray.
Used a pile of towels.
A toothbrush was foolish in his mouth,
small as his ordinary heart.
The mirror held but part of his face.
Whale eyes, kind and far apart.

Lips beautifully curved.
His breathing when I'd wake him
measured all the air in the room.

Women loved him
because he could barely be moved,
seldom dared. Safe as children,
they tried to hold on. One lovely blond
slept, sunbathing on the hairy, pocked
ledge of his back. Fun on the Riviera.
Beached in the local rag.

Once, posing outside The Garden,
he gently covered a pale one's face with his palm
as if to hide Beauty from too much light
or suffocate her laughter.
He loved Arabians, but never rode one.
All I have is pictures.

Him, in his last year, 47th, when he could
barely walk, clambering over the dinky chain
at Stonehenge, sitting on the swayed altar
as if it were an ottoman.

He was happy for days,
quiet as the beginning,
all that enormous
used furniture, nothing
to really wrestle with.

The Little Degas

Bronze, alert in a glass case, her fabric tutu stiff, she
could shift in a breeze. Chin up, wide, downcast mouth,
her narrow eyes appraise the class we imagine around her
as so much atmosphere, her feet turned out, yet to be
en pointe today, arms straight, stiff behind her perfect back,
expecting what seems a lifetime her chance to move.

What if she does? Makes us truly love her, desire
to balm and bandage her blistered feet, coo to soothe her
bondage among diaphanous ballerinas, hear her sigh
in the shadow of a decent, ordinary mother? Hovering father?

Could they want a daughter to see their faces reflected,
to ache to be that small, at rest in attitude, in bronzed laces?

She won't budge; we are safe. Her tiny, old, soft-metal eyes
"disdain to destroy us," ignore our heavy presence on her floor.

Mokule'ia

There were stars counting on you
to sense them.

— Rilke, *The First Elegy*

Barefoot on the seawall, you do look up,
though live stars flit in the slight surf.
Through flashy palm fronds, the constellations hold.
Silly Rilke. In the cottages, cartoon lights flicker,
citizens tuned to usual channels, Stars dancing.

A dog on the beach, black as a shadow of a shadow,
barks to stop the nonsense. The jewelry overhead,
big rocks, pass and pass and never touch.

Who should love their astral disdain
but the one serious drunk in the colony,
in a flamingo nightie, prancing like Isadora,
head tilted back, feet jamming sand,
her lipsticked rictus wide to the milky swarm,
scaring the dog back into the culvert?

Species

We didn't know to think, those first nights,
it was that luminous, moonlight playing
on rounds of hip, breast, biceps, glans.
We said our first words: "Stars," then "eyes."
And when palm fronds, twisting in dawn Trades,
loosed rags of light upon our briefly sated flesh,
it made no difference to the others,
stepping with cloven hooves, broad pads,
flying above or crawling to or from the sea
through rafts of wondrous bladder wrack,
that we hung back in shade, not shame,
to slow day's shaping so many others.

Mouldy Love

Do not lovers always
Overreach the limits of each other's lives,
Having promised distance, chase and home?

— Rilke

In the cave, the Crown Theater, I first saw Jane,
arched back on the grassy bank, shaking her wet hair,
laughing while Tarzan hauled himself
dripping from the croc ridden lagoon
with the same old rural grin,
Cheetah, jumping up and down, all gums,
screeching at the croc on Hero's heels.
I didn't care what happened to either.

It wasn't exactly love; Jane was too perky,
entirely too patrician, but it was a start
at competition, i.e. with that major fake,
Jon Hall, capturing the flashy eyes of Maria
Montez, in garish Technicolor, who captured me
with her lop-sided, sex-implicit smile and exotic
accent I now know was ordinary Mexican,
not Tahitian, or Arab. The one worse lover than Jon
was Victor Mature, of the goopy, spaniel eyes,
who strayed in a Biblical dream with Hedy Lamarr,
as much Delilah as I could imagine at the time,
but Montez made me stoic with ineptitude.

I recall in the serious foolishness of advanced age,
The Mummy's Ghost, when film life was all shadows,

my guy dragging his right leg (my hip titanium)
his left arm forward, hand in choke position,
still in rapt, mouldy love with Princess Ananka
(Ramsay Ames), oblivious to eons but ready
to annihilate any obstruction to past love
that I can share, in Kharis' case an apparent
re-incarnation: the skunk-locked secretary
in the Department of Antiquities, the old boy
infused by nine "Tana" leaves
simmered in a saucepan high in the ice-house
where he "slept," upright in a sarcophagus,
his servant-priest (John Carradine, later,
George Zucco in the sequel) stirring the wispy
brew, mumbling to his ancient deity, Osiris
I assume, folks always trying to find their way
back to sarcous life, that way, across the river.

Gabriel Garcia Marquez, thinking back
to his young years, of girls and women missed,
remembered a drunken, intellectual night, trying
for the essence of The Odyssey, concluded as "the fallacy
of nostalgia." The battered guy, afraid of sleep, talked
all night in the olive bed, already set upon leaving.
Dante had him say that he never came home at all,
but kept on going like Ahab, stumping along, another
"oudeis," fey angry flame in a Canticle Hell.
Sinbad was a happier soul, unlike Wilde,
no Oscar, just Cornell, poor actor.

I knew the priest had sent the loaded sarcophagus
up the ice-block conveyor to the top loft. I had
watched men saw, haul and load ice all one winter long
at Steven's Pond, the ice-house vaster than the Crown,
but no more full. An Egyptian in skimpy windings,
up in that gelid air! No wonder he was wry.

Ananka loved the Assistant Professor
(Robert Lowery) but something in her blood
longed for desert sand, evenings and muck
by the Nile, royal flirting at the edge of Kharis'
lower class gene pool, and with me, my frayed love,
tongue cut out by priests, as punishment
for yearning.

They've torn the theater down,
replaced it with virtual reality, a mall
that deep in moonlight might be fine
for shuffling along, three thousand years old,
looking at teen-age girls in hip-hugging shorts,

lower than the sarong Maria wore, little halters,
tattoos, and wanting to choke somebody,
especially the deity that placed me in this world
and they in theirs, as if I've been forever
in the movie house with old, gray stars, to choke
the entrepreneurs, the producers and directors
for violating the dark, peaceful tomb of recollection,
The Crown, in which I house my beloved
bitterness, first love, loves, imagining one
face at a time and vowing to find her,
somehow, among these young, pierced
embodiments, then chase, grab and carry her home,
sinking again with her in primordial gloom,
the toxic swamp behind the mall,
where no one will dig us for awhile.

Samson had it easy. He was as dumb
as his shoulders were square; his thought line
struggled in his plump lips, lax as his biceps,
armlets that would fit Delilah's ankles, dumb

as Tarzan, too, last seen romping in Pampers,
trying to yodel in Acapulco and looking for vines,
never to be born again, his idiotic buoyancy
belying ALS, disease the antidote to Jane's
charm … to not remember her name
or his real love's, Lupe Velez, who, deserting,
ran off with Gary Cooper in real time.

But that is all the past where the best movies
happen, that second to last scene, the English
patient, gathering her from the cave,
flying her mummy off in a Yellow bi-plane,
to crash into memory, like a dune, wind up
swaddled, tended by another Beauty, never to whiff
the sacred, nine "Tana" leaves.

Preparation

Walking carefully, quietly, upstream
then down, worn as stones in the brook
we used to leap, we peer, if blearily
at the bottom of things,
for anything.

A mosquito fish holds in the mild,
tidal current. Translucent shrimp,
sand fleas flick like nail parings.
Purple mussels huddle and periwinkles
glide slowly over stones, thick, green
heads of hair that stream erotically
from granite skulls, the brook
rinsing the meadow into the bay,
the tide returning the swell
nearly to the freshwater spring
while the beach reshapes, the brook
shifting gravel and sand, young curves,
thighs, shoulders.

Often as not she forgets, walks off
ahead of me, absorbing the saline,
amniotic light of morning. I am slow,
my knees taking pains to get along,
carping like gulls overhead, insulted
by our presence. So hard to walk
in unpredictable certainty.

Sometimes she'll turn to find me
stalled by the utter horizon
and knowing me reconciled

walks on as I recollect myself
to this understanding, old as salt,
the shore's wash, wedding.

III

Oasis

Noisy, insurgent mynahs
float down at dawn, screeching.
Red and yellow plumeria blossoms
drop in soft explosions and the local,
collarless stray trots by like Pharaoh's dog
with something on its mind.

When a breadfruit splatters, romantically,
the concrete walk, a nearby heart can
concuss on impact, pulp with fear, as when
love sours in a blur of flies.
Then the infant in the pool seeps *E. coli.*
And the Faithful are tourists.

It's all so utterly hopeless.
That's what my grandmother,
Edith Suontakanen, said in 1939.
She was still thinking of the shelling
of Hanko, of her husband, Johann,
out all night with his stoic *puuko,*
looking for Russians to knife,
munitions to blow in the dark.

She sat, croned, widowed at forty,
her mind an Estonian labor camp,
wry, arthritic fingers peeling her bunions
with his blade, her legs
wrapped in Ace bandage like The Mummy,
or sipping vodka with Finns in Quincy
also finding bliss not present
on Hancock Street in Uncle Ed's Elm Café.

Hearing shama thrush whistle on O'ahu
like breeze in a temple bell, I could
go dumb as a bud, shiver
to the bulbul's warble (they eat the hearts

out of orchids), go deaf to the last *la'a* chant,
or Walt's lilac ululation, to rockets
for the Year of the Dog, to rockets rising
from shattered cedars in Lebanon.

Agamemnon's Tomb

squats, a granite helmet,
short walk from the Lion Gate.
Inside, thoughts are bees beneath a chalice.
I want constellations, not this gloom.
I want Pegasus pacing Ptolemy's arena,
bears trudging… a crab, a scorpion
scrabbling a translucent shell, hell,
any size moon.

After all, eight feet into a Spartan tunnel
that women trudged for water during siege,
where spies slipped out and back at night
I'd heard a hymn, harmonic in a screen of green
flies, and froze, turned back, happy to travel
westward toward the future.

On Omaha Beach, shawled *ancien,*
Vichy, Resistance, sat beached in half-buried
canvas chairs, attended their small dogs
and mused on the Channel's oiled blaze, amused
by tourists trudging from the one upright bunker,
blinded and speechless, but relieved
by romance, the glistering history: a gray,
toy fleet positioned with a croupier's stick
on a sea-green table for forty, tiny red lights
for barrel flash, an audio-taped rendition of the volcanic
concussion of big guns, loud as the Beginning
and hallowed End, bodies washing ashore, boys,
men sheared by MP40 machine guns, precise
Karabiner 98K's.

I was still thinking of the Pantheon in Rome
that Spengler called "the earliest of all mosques,"
a hole in its head, a beam shining down over bent men,
eyes on geometric patterns in their carpets.
There, below one more marble Virgin,
Raphael and Maria's shadowed niche,
strewn with aging flowers art students toss.
They've already been in love.
The blinding absence overhead
flues a warm, ruined mind, the stone floor
a hard place for assignation, more
resignation … Conrad's "sacred inertia"
like the mendicant Brothers, past awe,
way past, shrewder than tourists

like me at Normandy, skeptically
content in the gaggle
hearing the recorded lecture's overture,
ein Schaferhund barking at the sea, June 6, 1944,
waking *Oberleutnant*, who, sleepy,
peered through slits in 8 ft. thick concrete
at the coming abstraction, 1100 steaming ships
before his face turned bright, as if he'd seen Helen.

English earphones cackling, a slow flag of
miscible causes waving in my stomach,
I conjured a mushroom revelation of the Nazi mind
snuffing the whole invasion, the tsunami
drowning the *vines de la Loire,* irradiating
oyster parks in *Bretagne.* Einstein told Roosevelt
the Germans were close.

I remembered so many capitols
with severe busts of men revered

or despised, some with eyeballs
blank with will and "dignitas"…some
with pupils drilled, later-minded men,
open to the lower world, and bored enough
to let light fly in.

St. Peter's, St. Paul's domes float,
light infusing warily the lens of censer-ed
atmosphere, smoky transepts
where one stares up with chary intention,
revealed in the unrevealing glow,

like a diver on the deck of the settled Arizona,
wraiths trapped inside, sixty feet down,
and looking up at loops of stars floating
among so many plumeria lei.
Every morning more seekers, eyes wide,
enter the sway-backed memorial,
or wander the decks of The Missouri,
as they do San Pietro in Vincoli
under stern Moses' ivory eyes, pupils
regressively set with the ferocity of Judgment,
lasers in the "world-cavern," where heroes
and wise men speak, blind with premonition.
Did Moses daven for revelation,

say, the Johnston Island blast?
July 9, '62, 800 miles south of 14,000 crosses
in Punchbowl Cemetery? Near midnight, ghoul
green light rose into the atmosphere,
x-rayed Diamondhead, Waikiki, Ewa and Waianae,
then fell in bloody runnels to the sea
while the few of us who came to watch
sat on our fenders and wept.
Doves, cardinals, mynahs sang for dawn.
And a child sang on a radio from Waikiki.

Perched on sandstone pedestals and ledges
in "la salle du frigidarium, gallo-romains du Cluny,"
shriven heads, no talking, whacked, toppled from west
lintels of Notre Dame, crashing on the stairs, the cobble yard,
expressions honest as concrete, seem to be listening,
within the perfect acoustics, for their own silence …
… maybe some passionate Latin, the Carmina Burana.

Patricia Lei Anderson, crowned Miss Hawaii, '62,
at the Waikiki Shell, for being beautifully bland,
sang *"un bel di,"* saw that night's dawn as glory

while well behind the Normandy beachhead
from easterly nations, *Gastarbeiter,* speaking in tongues
in tiny, bead-curtained rooms, were breeding again … new,
sullen life into the stale fervencies of Europe.
Another god rising?

Oberleutnant, in his wheelchair in Dusseldorf,
his teeth flowering in a pickle jar,
peers into his "gossip's mirror," mounted
on his window frame, back down the narrow street,
counting smocked Turks, arm in arm, swarthy
and illiberal, taking a short cut to the morning shift at Opel.

All that night I puked in one of the derelict bunkers
listing in the sand … suspect, delicious shrimp, snails,
vin rouge with mushy cork near Mont-St-Michel.
Altered by ammonia, the sweetening remains of my own
and others' urgencies, condoms and sticky shards,
a kind of peace rose in the hollowed me, feverishly happy
to hobble, coil, shaking, into the back of my '66
VW camper bus, to finally sleep off the constant,
explosive life of the species. But the next generation came,

revving and shrieking, swerving dirt bikes on the sighing dunes
till daybreak when another silence came.

I boiled coffee, tried bread, watched a pleat-faced crone
struggle down the ochre beach, her mutt
straining for a puffed gull with a twisted leg, for beer bottles
and plastic snack sacs like jellyfish. A man with beret,
slowly steering a beat-up green tractor, hauling a rake,
rowed sand into waves of wrack and trash,
the tines scratching at reaped souls buried there
when LSTs jammed in shallows on concrete teeth.
I thought of the Greek fleet, hauled out, wallowing
for years while Greeks killed each other, bored, in love,
waiting for Helen's gates to open.

The guide arrived, barefoot in her park uniform,
carrying her pumps, unlocked her attraction and joked,
"aus mit, Fritz," to the crone's terrier, that replied
by cocking his short, white leg of truce, drenching
the corner of the epic door.

Headed to war, Agamemnon's cranium burred,
rape his lying cause, and justice for his brother.
Victorious, home, he bathed in a marble tub.

Buses, tumid with sweet-sour diesel, heaved into the lot.
Old folks, arm in arm, women with fixed hair,
stagger to the graveyard, the bunker, the veterans
in peaked Legion caps, embracing,
moved to tears to see again the lethal site,
who, exhausted, were carried away by Mercedes
and Volvo, long, cushioned, air-conditioned caskets
within which old pains, like night-blooming cereus on O'ahu
opened, flush in the dusk of spirit, under half-moon
lamps above each seat, dusk for which I stayed

but not another day imagining ships, seeing so many
travelers enthralled by a light show, or *Oberleutnant's*
dove-gray uniform, hung on its tree
for these biddables to see, supposing he, stranded inland,
pushing his uppers into place, really had no story,
no love to tell.

The king's tomb, all that stone overhead,
dampened a bus load of teachers from New Hampshire
who bought slides of the gates, the tomb, to show
on a classroom screen, boring their Seventh Graders,
Briseis' age, barely young for love stories, the boys
verging on Patroculus' charm, busy, busy
with the spring trip to D.C., the promised Oval Office.

Hedgerow

Its easy green way between manors
or sober march edging Iowa corn
holds a thrush, a wren, a cackling pheasant.
Quivering setters in old cracked oils.
Shotguns popping Italian larks.

Hard to oversee these wicker bushes
dense as convention, more wall than guide
though one can walk this side assuming
pan pipes, sheep, maids and boys, classical
atrocities through the tragic tangle, fog of leaves
like Paul's glass with no lingo that tingles
and as for time it's time for tea, a beer,
time to bring the tractor in, wash up for supper,
bed, mucked boots by the door. Dogs arug.

Lately, but for occasional laundry, kites and blown
blossoms, hedgerows get less lyrically bedecked
with McDonald's boxes, plastic bags, white from Long's,
blue from Walmart, translucent from a produce aisle,
souls hanging on.

Children hear that hedgerows make neighbors
learn to be confidential and complaisant as refrain
or meter, rhymes that silence domestic dispute, rap, slams,
sirens roving moors, wailing in the burbs, leaping woods,

tastelessness diminished in their old lace
that cultivates the whisper, the chord reduced
fading out insurgent tongues, muting the noisy
International Harvester, engine of empire

plowing held acres of sacred armorial grief,
the blood of chivalry and Cherokee, grief
that inspires with luck some safe assignation,
some hint of Fragonard's pastel bliss, soft kiss,
quiet fuck.

Cezanne said "let the white shine through,"
yet filled the canvas as if to say "breathe irregularly"

the instant of birth, sneeze, gasp of orgasm,
flashing gaps in privet leaves
to glimpse a harmless world,
yet never covet.

Cool

Harnessed in imagos
like thoughts about animals,
dogs, bears, crabs, the hunter,
all lost in bleary, daylight blue,
they migrate all night long, brilliant
solos reflecting the immaculate
that seem to let us go
on with meditations, our
transcendental medications,
on loving, killing each other.

So breathe, lie back in the cool
bliss of the black lawn; pick one
beyond this galaxy if you can.
It could be gone by now, like a god,
its light arriving anyway, improbable
flicker in a detached retina, bit of ocular
migraine among the great shades:

father's black Buick Roadmaster,
or Roosevelt's cape, the way a manta ray,
exponentially cool to bitter wisdoms
gets larger in memory as it moves away,
mouth wide as Ella's
to brilliant, limbic systems of krill,
plankton and whale jazz, alto trills,
trombones swaying in spheres of instinct,
brain nuclei, wave shapes to applaud,
so cool, cool as night-wet grass
imagining your spine.

Another Sunday Morning

In the vast, near vacant parking lot,
a Volvo's window gapes, a hole
in pond-ice, edges pinked by dawn.
Gay wires bleed from the dash,
the mouth in rictus
where CD's sang

and the Electric Company
has failed for months
to fix the orange sodium lamp
that lit in benediction
a far row dumpster.

Cats hunt all night long, sleep now,
tired and coiled among the warming, gravid bags.
Pickup is Wednesday...

... not the end of the world,
just waste, the cats
in devotion to sex, garbage and rats
having missed a bundle of lavender feathers,
flesh smearing the curb in plum sacrament

where a peregrine, new to the city,
flared, stooped between the buildings,
tore a toxic pigeon from the air, then
dropped the carcass from a wind-blown ledge.
Raptors cherish innards
for quick energy...
... poor pigeon had been winging for the Florida
of St. Francis' hospital roof and powdery kin

huddled on sunny slate above the flash
of ice-roped eaves, thin-lipped over Exit 7.

Great Horned Owls

Blindness cured by dusk
they billow down, our minds
hooked to local news.

Rabbits and hares, lotus on the Ganges,
on brown open ground, try to get by
while a huge owl has lifted off a Yorkie,
raked air near an owner's ear in town.
The twisting dog, high above the roof,
captured by a cell phone camera.

Who doesn't love them, tall and lonesome
on vacant branches, hoo-hoo-ing
when we are trying to sleep, trying to mate,
as they are in the starred nights
sounding their long-drawn, hopeful arrangements.

Summer, moving north, they hunt skunks,
white runways down their spines and tails
easy prey clawing thawed lawns for worms.

But over ice and snow
during tarred nights, things
dive at our brains, whole
suburbs frightened by talons
big as a child's hand or idea of God
buried in our skulls.

Is this the beginning? A Yorkie? Cats?
Coyotes stalking infants in Sonoma.
A puma behind the garage.

Rats over-breeding. Gangs in alleys.
Snakes in the pool. A Kodiak bear
outside the French door. A girl's arm,
sheared by a tiger shark off Kauai,
that spits it out, not liking our blood, the iron in it,
an ape ripping off a guy's at the Denver zoo

and tossing it back through the bars
like a stick to fetch.
Rhinos rocking Hummers and Rovers.
Such essential humor ... bald eagles,
a working pair above the Wellesley campus
hauling off a senior. News.

Shh. Listen for the supple whoosh.
Watch for round, hard eyes that cannot move,
neck feathers like cigar ash.
Puffy detectives finding you out,
what you love and can't.

The Museum Of Natural History

In this dead, basement sunlight of Manhattan,
moose, elk, panthers in the diorama
look neither this way nor that, glass eyed

as in the foyer of the church in Antiquerra
Jesus on his hands and knees, small Iberian
original in polychrome, shadowed in a glass box,

seems more rare than happy.
So I kneel, almost the way he's down,
most of his way up Golgotha

his muscles olive roots, ribs raked,
femurs Byzantine, the sand dragged
as if by an exhausted turtle.

It's his face I come to see, no
animal we might revere,
every day for just a minute

sure of the sacristan's wonder
what this tourist is up to, twisting my neck
as if to find the leak.

His eyes are hot tar, hair derelict
(he might try to wash your windshield)
brow striped by the mesquite wreath.

The ruby drops are quite as
precious as they say, the skin
hauled against the skull by argument,

his nostrils flared with work, centuries of held breath,
bottom lip aggressive, about to speak, sell one true thing
I'm willing not to buy.

So I worry about the children, in white
flittering on the grooved stairs, around
a bride and groom consecrated
before a hooded camera on arachnid legs,
around the men, same black suits, the next week
who ant-walk a lofted, roach-colored case

down through the mumbling crones.
Kids who see their parents bearing yet
another infant up, out of the sun, into the gloom

right by Jesus to the blade of light above the font
among the Moorish columns, the baby
unswaddled, raw and screaming,

the water radiant ... dust,
smoke from the loopy censer
rising in the shaft.

Is it pain, or shame of the position
he got himself into? I don't think so.
The man's OK, no fool, and the children

pass with a dip of the knee, quick cross, quicker
than their *abuelas*, glad he's carried his this far,
whose eyes soften, as if to pat him on the back.

He too loves dust-free concentration
on what? Creation? Justice? Parents?
And the men outside, yawning,

wait for the corrugated door of the bodega
to groan open, roll night aside,
having risen for *café con Fundador*,

the local paper that confirms
nothing new has happened
because a man, about to snarl

at a blush of cuticle
tries to make his pinkie itch ...
cocked gold rattler in the elk's shade.

December 7

In pearl moonlight, brash white scarves
overpour the furthest reef, dousing the tinny
pulsing of my inner ear …
… then scritch, scritch at 0600 hrs., ninjas
scraping the cement with bamboo and steel tines,
raking the walk and gold dawn litany
of doves rueing, moaning albas,
shama thrush whistling wanton melodies,
mynah's screeching, the echolalia
baffled some by falling plumeria, soft
white and yellow propellers, and
vermillion poinciana blooms that,
crowning the tree, fire with first light
their pendant, funereal pods.

Then species all over the island run for shade:
buffo toads, be-dewed buddhas,
hop from immolation to safety
under the orange hibiscus, and black feral pigs,
humpy mongoose, roaches and centipedes
cross the highway toward rainforest
against the Michelins and Goodyears
hissing like samurai, downtown
to the rapture of business
while I listen for squadrons overhead.

Another assassin garrotes peace,
yanks the cord, adjusts the throttle
and marches a Honda off across the lawn
under a small blue cloud of exhaustion,
blades whirling, shearing, mulching

petals, leaves, pods and dog turd, *allegro multo*
to my annual hallucination: Zeros,
balsa bogies zooming in at 0800 hrs.,
antique torpedoes streaking in the blue,
their Doppler dozing into the legendary swish
of my evasion, an image of white wings
gliding toward a reef, out of fuel,
the Electra crumpled like a lotus,
a broken albatross, briefly on the ocean,
then the peace of subsiding, bubbling,
freeing Amelia, the American, to the gentle
wash of anemone between atolls. I begin
to doze, but

enough! Time to rise, to find a helical way to town
among the pile-drivers, mufflers and boom-boxes
that vibrate stapes and incus, tune all day
the vellum membrane of an aging *taiko*
to atonal confusion and otalgia, diffusing
notions of sanctuary, any nostalgia for paradise
beyond the terror in a scuba diver's rising vision
from the deck of the Arizona, the white, wavering,
sway-backed casket at Pearl
adrift in cloud and yesterday's lei.

Parasite

On the picnic table, the boy long,
striped blue fish, a *wahoo* laid open like a book,
spine, ribs and meat translucent vellum.
My blade slits the stomach for study.
Chartreuse juice, enzymes, run around
a half-digested *malolo*, flying-fish,
quiet as an impression of Triassic fern
traced from stone on onionskin.

In slow symbiosis in the matter
a walnut shaped flatworm, *Hirudinella
ventricosa*, exclusive to *wahoo*, crawls
safely in the soup that can digest aluminum
bottle caps. Pulpy, globular, color of clotted blood
it extends its "foot" on my palm,
the hook at the end picking my skin,
pulling the whole thing forward like a plan
quarter inch to a time as it did
in the belly of the fish … no Jonah,
just a vampire in the village.
A primitive that doesn't want to die.

Where is it going? To get out of the air?
Is it blind? Exploring new ground? Away
from light that shrivels and bakes it?

My father said I read too much into things.
But I troll these waters without hunger,
have caught and killed this five foot, fast
and lovely fish that will feed multitudes,
as I say, as I by impulse toss the wobbly pod
on the lawn like a child into the world.

Am I unsure about this changeling?
If I had halved it would it have re-divided,
multiplied as in a Friday midnight movie?

Things do happen. A shama thrush,
singer mimic, drops from the Plumeria overhead,
its breast the burnt orange of a Monk's robe.
It pecks at the thing in the grass, pinches it up,
flies off as if it knew it, or the new thing, too,
were beautiful.

Equinox

Cracked mug, black coffee
chrome yellow egg
at rest on toast
jam smear on faded china roses
a bent fork the usual
though today's a held breath
a slipped cog stalling the galaxy
when all things being equal
dawn sits honoring itself
bathes a pad of rotten snow
exposes spruce preaching silence
on the long shadowed hill
where the protesting spire
will impale the sun today
and be torched for that

Let It Be

Oaks and rumor approach the cliff
above the gaping quarry where work quit
when the men hit water. As if there were
a natural end to things.

We swam and dove until they banned it.
Polio. FDR. Fathers, older kids off to war.

People, dogs, cats always disappeared.
We said they sank.
I thought they might be summoned,
having seen Night of the Living Dead,
bleared by Schmidt's oval, ghoul-green
Dumont TV.

Now, homeless yellow fires,
down below the wind, flicker along its shelves.
Shapes drift from blaze to blaze, share
soup, booze, torn shoes, themselves,
flames glinting off shopping carts.

Quivering, because I fear height,
I glance down, sixty feet,
from this ledge of privilege
into summer's open wound,
ice-fast in winter, kids skating
lackadaisically on the lead lid.

I remember aerial photographs,
carbonized Hiroshima, Dresden.
I've seen the fresh lesion, relentlessly

healthy on Manhattan, trafficked by
furtive, bacterial need, pathed by
viral wealth, reminded by
occasional murder ... let it be,

site too sore to heal
under poured concrete and stainless
steel ... an ashy place, weeds
struggling, pigeons wheeling, no
mosaics for worn knees, no
vaults of solace or, god help us,
commerce.

Maundering the edge,
I imagine them risen, vague
by reflective pools, their own
engraved names, a crystal spire
infecting heaven,

but the theme is rubble after all,
subterranean voices hissing
air so harsh it keeps us raw,
coughing by fissures, toxic flare-ups
where people weep like candles,
no strophe, antistrophe,
just free to be resigned, finally,
faces in rictus lit by each other's,
vivid as the plastic flowers.

Green Flash At Hale'iwa Harbor

Light flicks from his long rod slicing air
to heave a three ounce lead
north toward the Aleutians.

Attached, a three foot drop-leader
ends with a silver circle hook, an amulet
skewering a strip of carmine *aku* belly or pallid
tentacle of *tako*, dancing deep in pellucid blue
for *ulua*, or smaller *papio*, flat, metallic crevalle
that hunt this water. On his rod a silver bell,
flashing while he waits for a tinkle and surge
as he sits on a white, 5 Gal. plastic bucket.

Finally, the little guy rises, reels in, ambles
south along the breakwater toward Ali'i Beach,
his shouldered rod springing black arcs,
bucket swinging like a censer
until he incinerates in sunset's saffron flares,
dropping to pink, while a quick,
lime-green flatline etches the horizon.

Burning The Furniture

We've settled in a bony house
nobody wants
a Victorian place with many rooms
Occupying one
we invite you to take another
though we have no food
have gone so lean we all seem tall
It will be fun this
self-sufficiency
eyeing each other

The refrigerator and two freezers
are vacant but for frost and mold
stained quilts kept from mice
No electricity
just three stoves one for wood
one gas and another kerosene
There is no gas no K1
tanks and cans light as heads with hunger
The young man who brings wood
has been on the way forever
may be at the war
so we burn the bedposts
the armoire chair-rails and finials
the banister

We plan for you the room
with fat sofa arm chair
a warm window facing south
where you'll be comfortable
if hungry and suspicious

We trusted everything global
cartoon gods ads the West
Switzerland and the Red Cross
but in this cold old house
we'll stick together
thin as pickets we also burn
thin as soup
heated by fallen twigs
varnished spokes rockers rungs
soup from melted snow
moldy hay a frozen
feral apple fungus
we break off like lip plates
from the north side of birch
with shrieks of bark

FSC
www.fsc.org

MIX
Paper from
responsible sources
FSC® C100212

Printed in June 2014
by Gauvin Press,
Gatineau, Québec

ACKNOWLEDGEMENTS

The James Dickey Review: "Still," "Snake"
The Long Story: "Great Horned Owls"
Valparaiso Poetry Review: "Making Me Look"
Aethlon: "Casting at Dawn"
The Sandhills Review: "Ripping the Traps"
Barnwood Press: "Oasis"
Wild Goose Poetry Review: "Preparation," "In Passing"
Cider Press Review: "Andre the Giant"
Alba: "Species"
Convergence: "Agamemnon's Tomb," "Mouldy Love"
Kaimana: "Cool"
Northeast: "Another Sunday Morning"
Salmagundi: "The Museum of Natural History"
Hawaii Pacific Review: "December 7"
Green Mountains Review: "Let It Be"
Ampersand Review: "Burning the Furniture"
The Chaffey Review: "At Dusk"
The Louisville Review: "Hedgerow"
The Hamilton Stone Review: "Just Over There," "Solace"
"Always After Fire"
The Chariton Review: "Equinox"

Some of these poems appeared in a chapbook, *I F*
Her Juicy, Thin-skinned Lemons, Finishing Line Press